WELCOME

D0131654

Bedrooms are nourishment for the soul. They're private retreats from crammed lives. They're the first view we glimpse in the morning and the last image we see before drifting off to sleep at night. Yet for all their appeal, bedrooms tend to get the short shrift in decorating, playing second-string to a home's public, more visible rooms. But why not dream—and do—big by giving personal spaces the attention they, and you, deserve? Imagine luxurious fabrics draping beds and windows, plush rugs underfoot, and sculptural furnishings that handle myriad tasks. The common thread of our featured bedrooms is that they epitomize luxury. Whether you're facing a master suite that's a blank slate, a guest room that multitasks as an office, or a child's room that needs to accommodate plenty of play, these bedrooms lend inspiration for melding functionality with grace.

The Editors

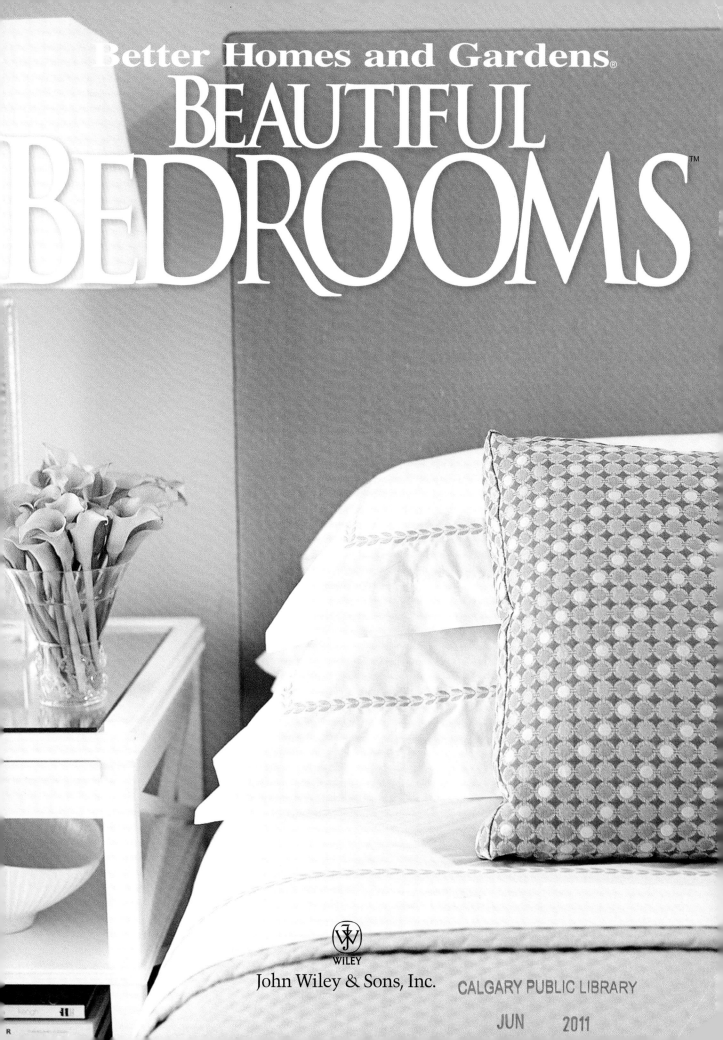

Better Homes and Gardens®
BEAUTIFUL
BEDROOMS ™

WILEY

John Wiley & Sons, Inc.

Published by John Wiley & Sons, Inc., Hoboken, New Jersey

Published simultaneously in Canada

For general information about our other products and services, please contact our Customer Care Department within the United States at (800) 762-2974, outside the United States at (317) 572-3993 or fax (317) 572-4002.

Wiley also publishes its books in a variety of electronic formats. Some content that appears in print may not be available in electronic books. For more information about Wiley products, visit our web site at www.wiley.com.

ISBN 978-0-470-48802-7

Printed in the United States of America

10 9 8 7 6 5 4 3 2 1

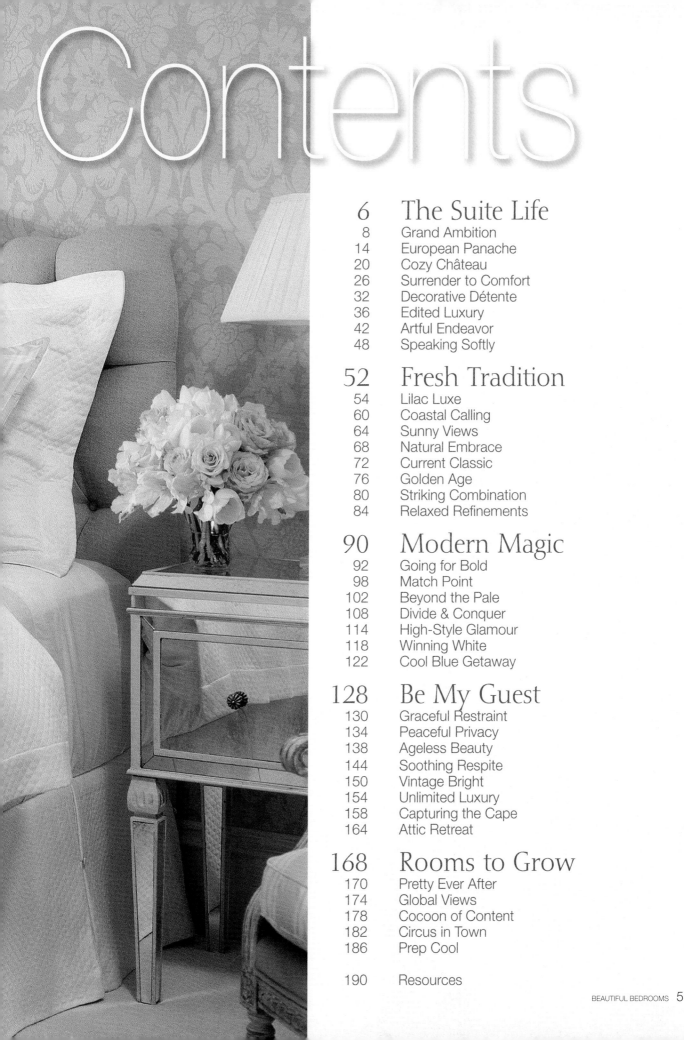

Contents

the suite life

Gone are the days of bedrooms designed purely for sleeping. Master suites are now amply sized and increasingly luxurious, outfitted with extras—from sitting areas and work space to entertainment centers, libraries, and spa-style bathrooms. With so many appealing amenities, master suites have become take-me-away destinations.

grand
ambition

Vision counts for more than size in this modest suite.

Grandeur comes to this bedroom and bath by means of a stately bed and hand-painted cornices that complement flowing silk panels. A pretty paint scheme, fine antiques, and ornate accessories complete the look.

"Whether a space is small or large, details make a room. They give the eye a place to land and linger—to ooh and aah."

—designer NANCY TAYLOR LYNCH

Luxurious and *dramatic* are words that come to mind when describing this Charlotte master suite. Yet the bedroom and bath started as so many do: just two plain spaces with 8-foot ceilings. Ordinary wouldn't suffice for the design team of Nancy Taylor Lynch, Christi Bowen, and Olivia Morgan. The designers wanted to create the illusion of grandeur "by extending the eye vertically," Lynch says.

The first larger-than-life move was the choice of the stately dark wood bed with a burnished gold canopy. The bed's commanding presence sets a regal tone. Grand touches continue at the windows, where custom hand-painted cornices lend architectural detailing. The cornices crown lush ball gown–like drapery panels that abut the pale yellow ceiling. Painting the ceiling this surprising color helps draw the eye upward, making the ceiling appear taller.

Walls swathed in a soft robin's-egg blue team with the yellow ceiling for "a lovely and somewhat unexpected contrast that supports the bed's starring role," Lynch says. The blue hue flows into the bath, where it shifts from paint to two wallpapers: an English floral print and a tone-on-tone stripe. Ornate accessories and antique furnishings further engage the eye. "You can put a lot of luxury and interest in a small space," Lynch says.

This photo: Paint and glaze artistically transform a standard vanity; sanding adds a timeworn look.
Opposite: A billowing pink silk skirt hides a humble plywood dressing table. The ornate mirror's size and style visually balance the bed.

european panache

Drawing on the European tradition of decorating with a mix of pieces, regardless of their pedigree, designer June Price uses a calming palette of soft blues, golds, and whites as a backdrop for showcasing the homeowners' antique furnishings. Now a comfortable haven, this small master suite invites lingering.

A perfectly matched bedroom appeals to many Americans. The dresser goes with the bed and the corresponding nightstand. And all the bedding comes from the same collection to ensure that the patterns and colors coordinate. But when charged with decorating this master suite in Atlanta, designer June Price looked to the homeowners' existing mix of furnishings, which included many French and English painted antique and reproduction pieces, for inspiration. "We used the furniture as a starting point," Price says. "We wanted the style to reflect a European flavor."

To that end, the bed features an eclectic blend of fabrics: a plaid bed skirt, matelassé bedcover, floral shams, and appliquéd throw pillows. The layered window treatments repeat the bed's rich texture as well as its warm gold, blue, and white color scheme. A sitting area, outfitted with plush armchairs and a cushy ottoman, snuggles up to a gas fireplace for more tactile comfort.

The room is capped by a dramatic vaulted ceiling. Price had it paneled in cypress wood and painted a subtle gray-blue to cast a calming influence over the room.

Pages 14–15: With its soft yellow walls, plaid and floral fabrics, and painted furnishings, this master suite bespeaks European elegance. **Above:** An antique chest and chair beside the bed provide linear contrast to the pooled linen draperies and a delicate floral needlepoint pillow. **Right:** Upholstered chairs and an ottoman gather around a carved stone mantel. The oil painting by Jacques M. Dunoyer is a treasured reminder of the homeowners' trip to France for their 15th wedding anniversary.

"Even though it's not a large space, we wanted it to be cozy and inviting, to encourage conversation and relaxation."

—designer JUNE PRICE

This photo: An antique painted writing desk and a rattan-back chair with a silk-covered seat complement the room's soft blue-and-yellow color scheme. **Opposite:** Attired in tasseled draperies and floral shades, the windows are formally dressed for any light occasion.

cozy château

Toile, wood beams, and a stone fireplace help designer

Barry Dixon transform a new suite into an old-world European escape. The designer's fine blend of antique and reproduction furnishings and his careful selection of timeworn accessories further hide any telltale signs of newness.

"I love the thought that you can linger in the room in the morning and have coffee, or retire to your room early."

—designer BARRY DIXON

Toile is one of those patterns with an uncanny ability to imbue a room with an instant patina. Interior designer Barry Dixon tapped its elegant old-world qualities to take the edge off this newly constructed Washington, D.C., master suite. He used the pattern generously, swathing the bedroom walls in paper-backed toile and repeating the same fabric in plentiful folds around the bed and windows.

Dixon neutralized what's often considered a feminine pattern by selecting a coffee-and-cream palette. The warm color scheme and his other deft design choices transform the blank slate into a cozy, character-filled European château that balances gender issues. Wooden beams that define the ceiling team with the toile for more timeless appeal. The stately four-poster is grand in scale, but its soft ribbonlike arches temper the masculinity. Dixon dressed it with simple fabric panels rather than using sheers or a canopy. A dark wood table and a carved wooden lamp contrast with a curvaceous porcelain lamp and antique charcoal drawing of a mythological goddess.

In the bathroom, Dixon employed a neutral palette of acid-washed tumbled marble tile, glazed cream cabinetry, and aged-plaster-look walls. "I think there's a yin and yang to the entire space," Dixon says.

Pages 20–21: The mocha toile bed curtains lined with tattersall checks are lush but not fussy. **Above:** The buttermilk-white finish on this chest contrasts with the dark hardware, carrying through designer Barry Dixon's balanced color scheme. **Right:** Rough-hewn beams define the ceiling and conjure images of a French château. Dixon stained some of the stone blocks around the fireplace with tea bags, others with coffee, to add instant patina. The stylized floral fabric on the chairs and ottoman provides visual relief from the toile walls and curtains.

Glazed cream cabinets
outfitted with dark hardware and bun feet introduce old-world charm to the bathroom.

Opposite: Upper walls that mimic the look of aged plaster visually soften and warm the bath's tiled surfaces, including the sunken whirlpool tub. **Above:** Built-in armoirelike cabinets offer storage space for linens and other bath essentials. The desk provides a quiet place for writing and also serves as a dressing table. **Right:** To create a unified look, Dixon framed the mirrors above the sinks with molding that matches the cabinets.

surrender to comfort

Enduring style takes more than beautiful fabrics, elegant furnishings, and a soothing palette. Designed by famed interior designer Charles Faudree, this master suite possesses these aesthetic qualities along with the comfort and practicality that make it inviting. With its desk, sitting area, and hidden entertainment center, this welcoming bedroom is made for living.

"We used reasonable fabrics where we needed lots of yardage and expensive ones for smaller areas. That gave us money to splurge on fringe."

—designer CHARLES FAUDREE

Master bedrooms are often treated as decorative leftovers. Even in elegant homes, they're often low or nonpriorities. "I see it frequently," says famed Tulsa interior designer Charles Faudree. "But your bedroom is where you start and end the day, so it needs to be restful, calming, and serene." Faudree wrapped this dreamy master suite in soothing blue and ivory for a couple who had never before decorated their bedroom. "Most people just need a little nudge," he says.

Using fine French antiques and yards and yards of lush fabrics, Faudree created a room with timeless grace and beauty. Striped silk panels cocoon a strikingly modern bed, and a pretty cotton floral moves from coverlet to classic draperies to a pair of antique club chairs. With cut velvet, leopard print, and muted damask thrown into the decorative mix along with richly detailed wallpaper and a soft-blue ceiling, this room is fresh and quietly lively. Smart furnishings, including a desk, a chaise longue, and seating next to the fireplace, make the bedroom comfortably appealing. Before Faudree lent his touch to the bedroom, it was strictly a place for sleeping. Now, his delighted client reports, it's a place to really live.

Pages 26–27: French garden tables make attractive nightstands that echo the contemporary bed's clean-lined metal posts. **Opposite:** The smallish bedroom window appears tall and stately with elegant traditional panels topped with valances hung at the ceiling. This gilt chaise came from a buying trip to France. **Above left:** A gorgeous French desk with cabriole legs and a Louis-XV chair provide a comfortable place to work, write, or pay bills. **Above right:** An antique Swedish chest is topped with fringed lamps and an opulent early-19th-century mirror.

The Musée d'Orsay

InfluentialInteriors

This photo: A luminous French armoire houses the television and stereo. Antique armchairs and an ottoman create a cozy and luxurious spot for reading or intimate conversation. **Opposite:** A handmade silk check shade with lush tassel trim crowns a humble distressed lamp. It's the kind of elegant detail that designer Charles Faudree loves.

decorative détente

Designer
Stephanie Wohlner
gracefully blends
traditional richness with
contemporary simplicity to cater
to the contrasting style preferences
of a Chicago couple. Soothing
neutral colors unify the look in this
master suite. The welcoming result
proves that a little give and take
can be a good thing.

New hardwood flooring and
a simple sisal rug add layers of warm color and interesting texture.

Keeping the decorating peace is all in a day's work for Chicago-area designer Stephanie Wohlner. Although she would decline to add marriage counselor to her résumé, Wohlner can easily lay claim to helping couples reach stylish design compromises that never give the appearance of settling for second best. Such was the case with Jessica and John Supera's elegant master suite. Jessica loves tailored interiors; John is more of a modernist. "There's a part of Jessica that wants chintz and toile, and another side that wants a dressier, more sophisticated design," Wohlner says. "But either way, she's much more traditional than John."

Taking on the roles of mediator and designer, Wohlner developed a harmonious design that weaves contemporary and traditional elements throughout the bedroom and bath. Neutral colors and clean-line furnishings are a nod to John's desire for simplicity and serenity. The damask wallcovering and the lamps, vases, and artwork that soften the setting have a decidedly feminine flair that suits Jessica's tastes.

"There are no fussy draperies or busy prints, so the rooms can appeal to both John and Jessica," Wohlner says of her creative balancing act.

Pages 32–33: Pictures of homeowner Jessica Supera's favorite sleeping spots inspired the design of the bed. "It's a perfect blend of masculine and feminine," Jessica says. "We love it." **Left:** The sitting area is comfortably outfitted with upholstered furnishings and an ottoman that doubles as a table. **Above:** Simply framed antique prints add a certain gravitas to the bath. The bench covered in buffalo plaid serves as a relaxed counterpoint to the artwork.

edited luxury

Creating a calm retreat long on classic

beauty and lean on color was furniture manufacturer Amy Howard's primary goal for the master suite in her new home in Tennessee. Clean-lined elegance, timeless profiles, and understated opulence combine with some brilliant surprises to make these spaces formal yet comfortable.

This suite signals furniture designer Amy Howard's move toward clean lines and a slightly contemporary spin on using old-world classics.

Pages 36–37: The Italianate canopy bed is dressed freshly in cream stripes and jacquards, and finished with glistening pillows encrusted with mother-of-pearl. The striking mirrored bedside tables are acid-etched and detailed in sterling silver gilt. **Opposite:** Midcentury-modern chairs near the fireplace are upholstered in sumptuous cut velvet. An old-world-style armoire lends quiet green, cream, and gold color. The crystal chandelier came from a Paris flea market. **Left:** Amy Howard chose a 1940s-style taupe mohair sofa to create sleek surprise and softness.

When furnituremaker Amy Howard designed her new home in Tennessee, she placed emphasis on creating a pared down, classically beautiful master suite. "I deal with color, fabric, and finishes all day long," Amy says. "I decided to make this my escape—quiet, restful, and nearly monochromatic."

Beige walls, reclaimed oak floors, a carved stone mantel, and deep crown moldings lay a serene foundation enhanced by textural Irish linen panels at the many tall windows. Amy went into the room with an airy mix of ancient, antique-inspired, and modern pieces that work together elegantly to promote calm. A spectacular 18th-century-inspired canopy bed is flanked by mirrored night tables. A 19th-century chest of drawers and old Venetian chairs lend rich patina. And unexpected modern pieces, including a pair of low-slung armchairs near the hearth and a supersoft mohair sofa near a hand-painted Italianate armoire that houses the television, provide freshness. "I wanted formality, but with a comfortable tone," Amy says. "I wanted the room to be refined, but in a way that was still welcoming. I want my family to come in and feel good here."

"The bathroom is inspired by what I love about fine hotels in Europe. It's a little slice of heaven here on earth."
—designer AMY HOWARD

Opposite: Amy designed the tall étagère for this space. She wanted the dark color and curvaceous profile as a contrast to the many hard lines and white palette. Its darkness echoes the iron chandelier and large ebonized mirrors above the sinks. **This photo:** Antique French panels framing the window slide shut to provide privacy. The oval tub floats in the room. "It's so regal. I've always dreamed of having a tub like this," Amy says.

artful endeavor

There's nothing abstract about designer Kathleen Navarra's daring approach to decorating this bedroom. The bold colors and graphic elements pay homage to 20th-century artist Mark Rothko. Like the famed painter's vivid canvases, the room catches the eye and sparks conversation.

"The furniture in this room appears quite contemporary, but it has classical roots."

—designer KATHLEEN NAVARRA

Filling a canvas with a few intense bands of color was a format embraced by Mark Rothko, who emerged in the 1940s as a leading abstract expressionist painter. It was with one of Rothko's hazy color-drenched artworks in mind that San Francisco designer Kathleen Navarra created this bold pink-and-brown master bedroom in a San Francisco showhouse. "My goal was to show that you can use color in a way that although on the outside may seem very bright and jarring is actually incredibly soothing and warm—just like a Mark Rothko painting," Navarra says.

Navarra painted the walls watermelon, topped with a brown glaze to soften the vivid hue and add depth. "It's a technique that appears in many Rothko paintings," she says. "He started out with a bright color and then put darker shades over it." The boldly striped upholstery covering two chairs in the sitting area is another nod to

Pages 42–43: The ripple design in the headboard and banding on the wool coverlet add graphic flair. Modern designs on the pillows play against traditional motifs on the drapery panels. **Above:** Texturally rich walls make the large room seem cozier, as do the velvet draperies that are hung from the ceiling. **Right:** The revamped fireplace gains a modern edge with a stainless-steel mantelpiece and mosaic surround. Ebony-stained floors accentuate the room's vivid hues.

Rothko's work, which often featured simple flat shapes. An embossed velvet in brown, pink, and red steers the room in a luxurious but still contemporary direction.

Neutrals instead of brights dominate the adjoining bath, where a mod oval-pattern tile mosaic in the shower stall adds verve. "I wanted people to walk into a room with a very contemporary edge to it," Navarra says.

Polished nickel fixtures,
a white marble countertop,
and chrome accents give the
bath its modern sensibility.

Opposite: A freestanding oval bathtub
nestles into an alcove outlined with beige tile
wainscoting. **Above:** Hand-carved mahogany
mirror frames with a nutmeg finish hide medicine
cabinets and play off the rippled headboard in
the bedroom. **Right:** Glass shower walls reveal the
eye-catching oval tile pattern in the shower stall.
To save space, the teak-and-chrome shower seat
can be folded up when not in use.

speaking softly

A quiet palette of pale greens, subtle blues, and creams creates an ideal backdrop for fine artwork and elegant accessories. Include a towering tester bed and a perfectly proportioned fireplace, and you have a master suite that doubles as a soothing sanctuary. Draperies, hung at the ceiling, reinforce the luxe look.

Pages 48–49: The gracious master bedroom incorporates a towering ceiling, pale green walls, a cream-color carpet made of linen and silk, and silk drapes with subtle green and charcoal stripes. **Left:** Jane Schwab commissioned the queen-size canopy bed from a local Charlotte artisan, who adorned the frame with painted chinoiserie designs. The headboard is upholstered in a light green strié velvet. **Opposite:** The brown marble fireplace "is taller than most because of the ceiling height and the size of the room," Jane says. The designer rarely uses mirrors above fireplaces but fell in love with this rosewood piece because of its shape.

Before interior designer Jane Schwab began planning the interior of the newly added master suite in her 1923 English Colonial home, she took measure of the room's fine proportions and natural light. To play up these stellar features, Jane settled on an understated blend of light greens, blues, and off-whites. She added sizzle to the elegant mix through her careful choice of furnishings—foremost among them a towering custom canopy bed painted with chinoiserie motifs.

Beneath one window rests a comfortable settee upholstered in linen of the palest robin's-egg blue. A pair of French-style bergère chairs from her husband's mother and a small bench that hails from England define the seating area by the fireplace. "I spend a lot of time there reading in the evenings," Jane says. "It's such a comfortable spot."

Thoughtful editing of accessories makes the room's vignettes all the more appealing. Bedside tables boast wooden lamps with natural-color pleated silk shades along with a few interesting objects, including two petite antique cast-concrete birds. Above the bed hangs the painting *The Yellow House*, a pastel by New England artist Mary Loring Warner.

"The colors she used were just wonderful," Jane says. "In general, the right colors are just so important, especially in a bedroom."

fresh tradition

f Fine furniture, luscious fabrics, and personal treasures are hallmarks of traditional style. Today's bedrooms embrace those elements in exciting new ways. The look is relaxed and uncluttered, with clean-lined accents often pulled in for an element of surprise. Of course, fresh tradition still translates into timeless and classic.

lilac luxe

This opulently chic bedroom by British interior designer Nina Campbell is a celebration of lilac, which she considers one of the most calming colors in the rainbow. Complemented by creamy whites, crystal, luminous antiques, and a magnificent mirrored headboard, this is a room that is as rich as it is relaxing.

"Lilac, as a color and as a scent, is conducive to calm. It is a perfect backdrop."

—designer NINA CAMPBELL

Lilac blooms ever so brilliantly in this sophisticated bedroom concocted by famed British designer Nina Campbell. "Lilac, as a color and as a scent, is conducive to calm," Campbell says. "It is a perfect backdrop for a bedroom." The stunning cream-and-lilac striped fabric upholstering the walls was the starting point. The jaunty fabric sets a glamorous tone enhanced by a showstopping canopy bed mirrored on both headboard and footboard, a glistening mother-of-pearl dressing table, and luminous dark wood antiques. The boldly scaled floral silk that hangs in long, gently folding panels at the windows is another recent Campbell design. "It was the first time I had done printed silks and I was dying to use them," she says. Campbell gathered the shimmering draperies on whimsical acrylic rods that are barely there but still shine brightly. Antique lighting—a chandelier with glass beading, crystal vanity lamps, wall sconces, and a pair of rococo candelabra—lend history, sparkle, and lovely light that make this utterly romantic room glorious every day and every night.

Pages 54–55: In her debut appearance at the Kips Bay Boys and Girls Club Showhouse in New York, British designer Nina Campbell used lilac fabrics of her design to fashion a bedroom that exudes Upper East Side glamorous style. **Left:** A creamy silk chaise nestles up to a mirrored folding screen and a French bombé chest near the bedroom fireplace. Dark-stained floors ground this airy space.

This photo: Paintings, Biedermeier tables, crisp white bedding, and a pair of electrified antique candelabra add to this bedroom's luxurious mood. **Opposite:** A curvaceous mother-of-pearl dressing table strikes a sumptuous pose next to tall windows draped in shimmering printed silk. A diminutively striped silk dresses a sleek modern dressing stool.

coastal calling

Blessed with a gorgeous water view, this Rhode Island bedroom is all about understated elegance. Designers Gary Gesualdo and Annie Burke took their cues from the views outside, building a palette of cool whites and light greens. The white finish adds seaside appeal to the four-poster while shell artwork contributes appropriate accents.

The soft green walls, painted
with a ragged finish, add depth to the under-the-eaves space.

Pages 60–61: "The bed was a huge inspiration—after that, everything fell into place," designer Gary Gesualdo says. **Opposite:** Texture, rather than color, on the chair adds interest to the reading corner. **Left:** The soft green stripe on the bolsters mimics the wall color. **Below:** A welcoming pineapple motif can be found on the drapery rod finials, and are also on the posts of the bed.

The scale of the beautiful maple four-poster—called the Portsmouth Pineapple—made it perfect for this showhouse bedroom. "It's a popular style for this area," says designer Gary Gesualdo, owner of East Coast Designs. He and co-designer Annie Burke favored the short posts for the 14×17-foot room, and the bed's traditional feel matched the mood of the Shingle-style home. They lightened the look by having the bed glazed with an antique finish.

The custom damask duvet cover and matching pillow shams distinguish the bed as the room's focal point. A symmetric arrangement of pillows in coordinating fabrics creates the finishing touch.

Gesualdo and Burke selected soft green walls painted in a ragged finish to give the room depth—especially important with the low, slanting walls of the under-the-eaves ceiling. Sheer Roman shades and silk drapery panels hang softly at the French doors and large windows; the handmade wool-and-silk Iranian area rug in a subtle floral print introduces a warm touch to the cool scheme.

sunny views

Traditional furnishings strike a delicate balance

between grandeur and youthful appeal with a light and airy approach in the San Francisco Showcase bedroom designed by Tish Key. Swathes of sunny yellow fabric, an abundance of checked patterns, dressmaker details, and painted furniture create a lively mood.

"The room is sophisticated enough and neutral enough to be timeless."

—designer TISH KEY

Pages 64–65: Hand-painted with a charming floral motif, the Italian bed is surrounded by flowing silk bed curtains that create a special room within a room. Interior designer Tish Key balanced traditional lines with light, playful colors and fabrics. **Left:** Key designed the sitting area with everything needed for relaxing or reading. A soft yellow linen-velvet love seat, flanked by built-in bookshelves that display an ever-changing array of personal treasures, provides the ultimate seating. Hand-painted flowering vines and birds are sprinkled throughout the room. **Opposite:** Bed hangings frame a view of the pretty skirted dressing table adorned by a classic triple mirror.

Furnishing a bedroom can be quite an investment, especially when the setting is as grand as a former British consulate chosen for the San Francisco Showcase. To do justice to the classic architecture and large-scale space, interior designer Tish Key came up with an enduring bedroom that put classic good looks above trendy style.

She approached the spacious, high-ceilinged room by acknowledging its need for large-scale, important furniture, designing a bed fit for the room's proportions and including a separate sitting area with tufted sofa, coffee table, and comfortably upholstered chairs. The Italian bed, hand-painted in a floral motif, definitely stars in the pretty scheme. With a stately canopy, its yards of fabric gather in a center rosette and flowing bed curtains. Creamy painted finishes give French-inspired traditional furniture a fresh, updated look. A trumeau mirror, leaned casually on the mantel, and crystal chandelier add just the right touches of glimmer.

A glowing golden-yellow palette complements the light-filled space, accented with touches of pale seafoam green. Yards and yards of checked fabrics define the room with youthful cheer—from the tufted seats on the armchairs and the frilly silk vanity skirt to the full-length draperies and bed curtains. "The room is sophisticated enough and neutral enough to be timeless," Key says.

natural
embrace

Glass walls erase the lines between
indoors and out in this La Jolla,
California, master suite. Added
as part of a major remodeling
to the 1920s home, the cast-
concrete fireplace and raised
hearth warm the private retreat
on cool coastal evenings and
winter days and appear to float
in the magical space.

Beautiful in its simplicity, this master suite addition

opens the home to one of its most engaging features, an interior courtyard surrounded by trees and flowers. The vaulted ceiling and French doors to the garden further expand the openness.

Architectural and interior designer Holly Hajjar Lorah planned the master bedroom as part of a major renovation that updated and expanded the home. With such strong architecture and incredible views, the homeowners wanted to keep the overall palette and decorating scheme relaxed yet romantic. Nothing in the room competes with the splendor of the courtyard. All the colors are soft neutrals, but they appear in a multitude of textures, including the wispy lace swags at the small windows beside the bed and the punchy leopard print on the foot-of-bed bench. Smooth white armchairs can

Pages 68–69: In the midst of a wall of windows, a floor-to-ceiling fireplace creates a focal point. **Opposite:** Resting against the small canopy, three European shams serve as a comfortable headboard. **Above:** Floor lamps illuminate the armchairs in the sitting area, making them cozy reading spots. Unmatched tables provide anchoring dark accents and places to set a drink.

snuggle up to the fireside on a chilly evening or offer a spot to enjoy the California sunshine.

With no window treatments softening the space, a bold striped canopy over the king-size bed takes over the duty. The pattern repeats in a smaller version on the bedside chests. Throw pillows on the bed and a needlepoint rug complement the green scene outside the glass.

cur.rent classic

Making traditional decor lively and livable is Atlanta interior designer Dan Carithers' stock in trade. Known for a light touch with pedigreed antiques, he demonstrates his prowess in this graceful master bedroom adorned with classic furniture, timeless toile, and a modern-day freshness that comes from knowing when to say *when*.

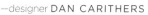

"All rooms ... should feel alive, not static. . . . I can't stand a room full of brown furniture. This feels so much better."

—designer DAN CARITHERS

Pages 72–73: This master suite's warm, sun-drenched mood makes 18th-century-style furniture feel at home in the 21st century. **Opposite:** A restrained palette and subtle pattern play make the blue-and-white toile dynamic. A classic sunburst mirror provides a touch of opulence. **Left:** Faux-tortoise mirrors lend richness. Swing-arm lamps mounted inside the bed curtain are detailed with delicate blue fringe.

Interior designer Dan Carithers is passionate about 18th-century style. Yet this master bedroom graced by a mahogany four-poster, Chippendale sofa, fauteuil chairs, Regency coffee table, and blue-and-white toile fabrics is no stiff showcase for expensive antique furniture. "I always try to do something to introduce a difference and a humble quality," Carithers says. "All rooms, including those with very fine furniture, should feel alive, not static."

Carithers brings modern-day vitality to historical style in subtle ways—it's in his colors, finishes, pattern play, and attention to light. The beige-on-beige striped wallpaper is understated but creates architecture, a tailored feeling, and coziness. Warm woods—in the bed, a mirror, and a table—and neutral wool carpet on the floor imbue softness and comfort. Set against this restrained backdrop, elegant blue-and-white toile dressing the windows, sofa, chairs, and bed curtain is strikingly fresh and vital. Carithers' decision to paint his client's mahogany sofa and armchairs white was among his most important. "I can't stand a room full of brown furniture," he says. "This feels so much better."

golden age

Feminine is in. Saccharine is not.

Designer Chris Garrett strikes a sweet balance in this master suite. It is decorative but not froufrou, delicate but not effete. Capitalizing on the room's ample sunshine, she uses light, bright colors, silky fabrics, and the sparkle of gold to create an environment comfortable for him and a true haven for her.

Natural light is an interior designer's best friend. And with three window walls, this bedroom invited Chris Garrett to create a master suite where sunshine would reign supreme. "I took full advantage of the room's very best attribute," Garrett says.

Light wasn't all the Chicago-area designer had to work with. The well-proportioned room boasted high ceilings, commanding windows, hardwood floors, and a neoclassical fireplace mantel. Garrett's mission was to make this room feminine but not fussy, polished but not stuffy. She began with mustard-yellow walls, bright white trim, and almost-black-stained furnishings. A tall four-poster, matched side tables, and a spacious desk possess traditional lines but strike daringly dark silhouettes in this airy, sun-soaked space. "I wanted to create some drama but still be timeless," Garrett says. Fabrics play to the room's sunny glow. A golden-tone coverlet

Pages 76-77: Touches of gold, including detailing on bedside tables and a casually propped gilt mirror and overlapping painting on the mantel, play harmoniously to the understated opulence. **Opposite:** An ample desk with plenty of drawer storage is a practical and serene place to pay bills, write letters, or work on a laptop. **Above:** This gorgeous mural is original to the space. Designer Chris Garrett augmented its exotic air with an old Chinese chest with its own rich patina.

softens crisp white bed linens, and shimmering yellowish gold silk adorns windows in the form of pinch-pleat draperies at the French doors and lush balloon shades at smaller windows. "I chose smooth textures and pale colors," Garrett says, "because they are so elegant when streaked by sunlight."

striking combination

Pretty in pink is the mantra for this master bedroom. An Atlanta design team partnered hot pink with creamy white for a fresh look that is surprisingly peaceful and sophisticated. A mod fabric art piece and dramatic draperies play up the lively color scheme.

"The pink isn't as predominant as you might think. The atmosphere is more serene and calm after you've been in the room."

—designer MEEGAN JOWDY

Pages 80–81: Fabrics mounted over canvas stretchers screw together to form a mod art piece; metal picture hangers suspend the lightweight wall hanging above the bed.
Opposite: Antique French armchairs mingle with a Plexiglas table, frosted pink lamps, and an Art Deco-inspired sofa. **Left:** The metal drapery rod continues around the room as a picture rail.
Below: A cream-and-pink striped fabric was used for the draperies. The edges of the cream stripes are sewn in 10-inch-wide box pleats at the top, causing the pink stripes to gradually flare.

Color—hot pink to be exact—is the first thing that comes to mind when glimpsing this master bedroom in an Atlanta showhouse. To designers Meegan Jowdy and Bob Brown, however, the room is more about how a neutral foundation needn't bore with blandness. "I didn't want color to be primary," Jowdy says. "I wanted to have an overall neutral background with punches of color."

The walls, trim, furnishings, and fabrics all display shades of cream that establish a sophisticated, peaceful ambience. The pale walls serve as a gallerylike backdrop for artwork—most notably the fabric collage that takes the place of a headboard. Pink fabrics mounted on canvas stretchers overlap one another to form a large geometric design on the wall behind the bed. "In essence, we've used fabric as art," Jowdy says of the eye-catching work that gives the room a distinct modern attitude.

Though the collage is the room's tour de force, other vivid elements are at work. Pink appears in accent pillows, window treatments, lamps, and a custom-dyed area rug that links the sleeping and sitting areas. Ultimately, the creamy neutral hues keep the pinks in check, ensuring that the bedroom is a restful place.

relaxed refinements

Fine traditional
design is in
the details, which is
why this compact guest room in
a New York apartment displays
beauty from floor to ceiling.
Nothing is overlooked, from the
finely fabricated, goblet-pleated,
and trimmed drapery panels
to the matching damask-motif
wallpaper. Even the bed offers
supreme, crawl-in comfort.

Pages 84–85: Brown and tan accents—in measured amounts—give the furnishings prominence against the blue-and-cream backdrop in this handsome guest room. **Opposite:** A small antique table serves as a decorative and space-saving bedside table. **Left:** Timeless traditional drapery panels dress the window. Panels are pulled to the side to let in natural light, often a luxury in a city apartment. The striped wallpaper in the concave molding tucked just below the ceiling complements the damask pattern.

Designer Marshall Watson balances the fine furnishings and exquisite finishing details of traditional interiors with today's light palettes and thoughtful editing. His work, as this guest bedroom illustrates, denotes classic style in imaginative ways. Despite its diminutive size, Watson gave the room grand importance by dressing both the window and walls in an overscale matching damask print. Upholstered walls soften every inch of the space. The graceful window treatment is subtly tied back to put the focus on the city view and show off the dressmaker details. The pleated goblet header dresses the part with complementary covered buttons, and a beaded braid fringe cascades down the panel's leading edge. The nearby golden headboard features deep tufts and tailoring suited to the sophisticated room.

Watson carefully chose the finishing touches to complete—but not overpower—the serene blue-cream-toffee color scheme. Individual lamps, rather than a matched pair, add interest, as do the bull's-eye mirrors hung from the picture molding above the bed. Minimal accessories leave bedside space for books and glasses.

Details wrap guests
in ultimate comfort while
treating them to elegant style.

Opposite: Light from the window bounces off the many delicately reflective surfaces, such as the bedside lamp and luminescent bed fabrics. **This photo:** Fresh hydrangeas share the blue hues found throughout the bedroom.

modern magic

Sensuous and au courant, modern bedrooms emulate the best of high-style boutique hotels where sleek furnishings and well-dressed beds welcome the most discerning guests. Add the creature comforts of a discreet television, a dressing area, and a spa bath to create the ultimate sanctuary for private relaxing and recharging.

going for bold

With royal purple setting the sumptuous tone, a striking palette and glamorous furniture make this master bedroom as exhilarating as a luxury hotel suite—but with all the sink-right-in comforts of home. Mirrored bedside tables, a decorative chandelier, and collected mercury glass multiply the high-voltage style.

Relying on multiple hues
of the same plum color makes this room rich and glamorous.

Pages 92–93: Layered bedding and accent pillows contribute high-impact (and easily changeable) accents to the design scheme. **Left:** An occasional chair, teamed with a small round table, provides an elegant spot for reading or putting on shoes. **Below:** Art Deco-inspired accessories, including a vibrant sunburst mirror, amplify the allure of the wallpapered alcove. **Opposite:** Reflective surfaces, including mirrored bedside chests and a mercury glass lamp, reflect natural light—a plus on overcast or winter days.

Designer Doug Hansen went for bold in this master bedroom, choosing purple walls, richly grained wood furnishings, and sparkling mirrored accents. And he did so without sacrificing comfort or practicality. While the room is undeniably glamorous and sophisticated, it also benefits from ample storage, softness underfoot, and areas to relax. Classic furniture makes a big statement while avoiding design trendiness.

The sleigh bed, with its rich grain and transitional elegance, gave Hansen his savvy starting point. Even if the rich purple walls become a passing fancy, the bed will adapt to any color scheme and any design style from contemporary to traditional. The coordinating dresser, handsomely showcased in an alcove between the room's windows, is also timeless and perfectly scaled. The decision to wallpaper that alcove in a gold floral vine pattern on a deep purple ground gives the wall the stunning impression of high-impact artwork. It also plays nicely with the mirrored bedside tables, mercury glass and Lucite lamps, a sunburst mirror, and shimmering bedding. A magenta chaise, an imitation suede screen trimmed in nickel nailheads, and a giant-scale floral rug atop wood floors introduce warmth and comfort—along with a happy, healthy dose of whimsical flair.

Shimmer gives everything from fabrics to furniture a sensuous flair.

Above: The rich grain of the bowed chest gives the modern piece a formal look. A pair of clear lamps adds style without introducing competing color. **Left:** A beaded chandelier over the chaise has decidedly feminine appeal. **Opposite:** A dark eggplant-hue folding screen and a magenta chaise exemplify the feel of Hollywood glamour.

match point

Color couples such as black and white have legendary status. And for good reason. They're easy to use and have a clean, high-style look that endures. The ultimate contrast translates into the perfect duo for a no-fuss, tailored bedroom. This master takes hold with a dark bed dressed to impress in stark white linens.

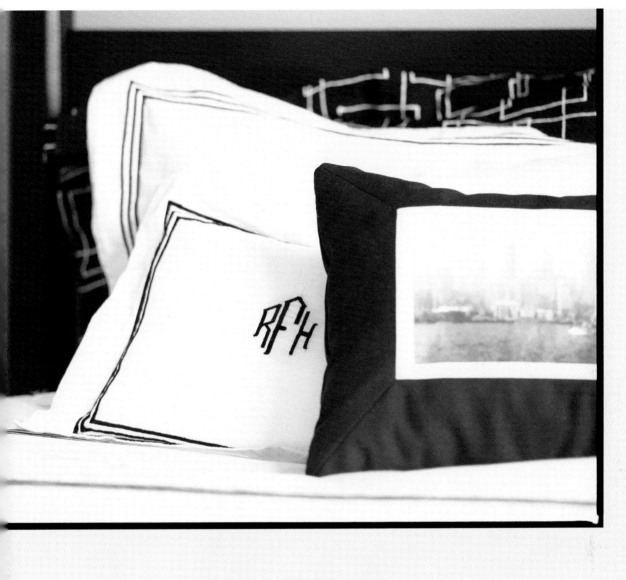

Black and white rule. If you want it fast and you want it to last, this tried-and-true pairing is tailor-made for you. The combination never falls from fashion, and a crisp and classic look is just a few furnishings away. Del Mar, California, triathlete Bob Fleet knows. He turned his light-filled master bedroom into a chic master suite with an easy two-color palette and a little help from decorator-friend Paula Stein.

Bob skipped window treatments in favor of natural light. He painted walls warm beige and the trim and ceiling bright white, and he laid creamy carpeting underfoot. To this serene backdrop he added bold ebony-stained furniture, including the contemporary four poster that is the room's centerpiece and a footed bench detailed with a Greek key motif. A pair of side

Pages 98–99: Tall, unadorned windows set a handsome, clean-lined tone. **Above:** The bed's pillows provide important pattern in this quiet space. Monogrammed shams combine with bold geometrics and a black-and-white photographic pillow to provide an essential touch of whimsy. **Opposite:** An oversize shell and tall vase provide sensual curves in a room dominated by hard lines as seen in the bedside lamps.

tables with marble tops echo the heavily veined look of the nearby fireplace hearth. To keep things interesting, a raffia upholstered armchair and graphic bed pillows lend just enough pattern, but not so much that they interfere with this room's glorious serenity. "This look is perfect for me," Bob says. "It fits my lifestyle hand in glove."

beyond
the pale

An ethereal palette, alluring shapes, and shimmering finishes combine gracefully to create a modern suite where opulent high style is whispered rather than roared. Traditional touches temper the modernity, and a distinctive headboard creates a glamorous focal point. The headboard also creatively doubles as a wall, turning the large space into two cozy areas.

"Layering window treatments creates comfort and calm. Two sets of creamy panels amplify warmth, softness, and understated luxury."

—designer BARRY DIXON

Serenity reigns in this quietly glamorous modern suite where colors caress, fabrics are soft and silken, and amenities abound. Washington, D.C., interior designer Barry Dixon wrapped the room in a palette of celadon, pearl, mist, and gray-blue-green. "I chose the colors of fog to create cloudlike calm," says Dixon, who was careful to ensure calm wasn't comatose. "A master suite should be sexy," he says. "I wanted this room to be luminous with an understated opulence."

The tufted-silk headboard that makes the bed this room's focal point ensures that status. It also has a practical raison d'être: creating two cozy spaces from a single room that was just too large. Trimmed in nailheads and framed by petite mirror-encrusted night tables, the silk-dressed bed is positioned with a view of a chic sitting area and a flat-screen television mounted on a side wall. The television is revealed when a large mirror decorated

Pages 102–103: A misty palette establishes relaxed serenity. A sensuous quality comes from a silk headboard and a blend of finishes. **Above left:** A track-mounted mirror slides to reveal a flat-panel television. **Above right:** Pink flowers give the muted scheme a hint of color. **Opposite and page 106:** Sitting-area fabrics are soft and monochromatic. **Page 107:** A mirrored demilune table sits beneath the oval "window" on the other side of the pseudo wall that creates two intimate spaces.

with antique bookplates is slid to one side. Three layers of window treatments and a sea-grass rug lend warmth and relaxed texture. Delicate touches of shine introduced by a glass floor lamp and side table, chunky beads on a pendent chandelier, and softly shimmering upholstery fabrics heighten the room's comfort, richness, and elegantly modern allure.

"A beautiful bedroom is not an indulgence, but rather a smart investment in well-being. To build a room you will want to live in for years to come, a quiet palette is a good place to start."

—designer BARRY DIXON

divide & conquer

A smart floor plan and sleek
East-West furnishings give a long, narrow room broad new appeal as a serene master suite. A daring combination of zesty orange and dark chocolate gives the space visual punch. The lively saturated hues also pave the way for designer Rob Horby's eclectic mix of mod and Asian elements.

"I wanted to show people how good orange can look. It's a bright, happy color that brings energy and life into a room."

designer ROB HORRY

A less confident decorator might simply have walked away from the 40-foot-long room in this San Diego showhouse, but not designer Rob Horby. "I've always liked a good challenge," Horby says. He also had a plan—to divide and conquer.

By sectioning the long, narrow space into three distinct areas and linking them with an orange-and-brown palette and a sleek mix of Asian and contemporary furnishings, Horby created a sophisticated master suite with wide appeal. "I envisioned this as a place where you could close the door and be away from the family," he explains. "I wanted this to be a real adult retreat."

At one end of the room, a pair of chaises forms a cozy spot for watching the television, which is tucked inside

a 19th-century Chinese persimmon-red armoire. At the center of the room, Indonesian chairs and a large drum coffee table nestle up to a fireplace, providing a place to unwind with a glass of wine and a good book. Just beyond, the sleeping area is anchored by a sumptuous brown suede platform bed with a tufted headboard. The layered bedding echoes the richly striped curtain panels at the room's windows.

Horby used an abundance of Asian antiques—such as pieces of a *tansu* chest, which are used as bedside tables and as a foot-of-bed bench—to balance the modern mood of the space. "Asian antiques lend freshness and serenity to any room," Horby says. "Their clean lines make them perfect in contemporary settings."

Pages 108–109: The antique *tansu* chest sections that frame the bed are sleek, but they also provide practical, easy-access storage. **Opposite:** A silk scarf suspended from a rustic piece of wood adds a splash of color behind a neutral chaise. **Above left:** A Tibetan rug anchors the sitting area, dominated by an antiqued fiberglass mantel that showcases luminous orange and brown pottery. A mixed-media "quilt" above the mantel features handmade postcards tucked into plastic pockets. **Above right:** The bamboo screen behind this chaise was made from three vintage sliding panels.

Once used as transoms in Japanese houses, carved 1930s *ramma* panels above the bed serve as contemporary Asian artwork. Teak lamps and the suede bed echo the deep tones of the *ramma* frames, providing a handsome contrast.

high-style glamour

Recalling the movie-star allure of the 1940s—when the heroine always brushed her hair at a dressing table—this chocolate-and-rose bedroom illustrates the softer side of sleek, sophisticated design. A bed dressed in luxurious, gown-inspired silk bedding reinforces the Hollywood cachet.

Luxurious bedrooms often start from the ground up. "A beautiful rug is a great place to start," says decorator Elizabeth Roeder. Her inspiration for this bedroom for the Vassar Show House in Philadelphia began with a Persian carpet that provides warmth atop hardwood floors and also establishes a rich palette of chocolate, rose, caramel, and moss. "Some people want light, airy bedrooms and some people want a cozier feeling. I went with a cozier feeling that's conducive to relaxation and sleep," Roeder says.

The large-scale, stylized floral pattern of the rug also invokes a transitional tone. "I didn't want an overly traditional look and I wasn't interested in contemporary," Roeder says. "This sets a perfect mood that's comfortable but still a bit glamorous."

Roeder plucked a rosy hue from the rug to repeat on a tall, tufted silk headboard that provides this room's glistening focal point. She then painted walls caramel and dressed the bed in a lustrous mix of silky linens. Dark-stained furniture, including a pair of handsome chests framing the bed and a pretty vanity topped with three curvaceous mirrors—a shape echoed in the nearby chair—gives the room an air of movie-star sophistication. "It's lovely to repeat shapes as well as colors in a room," Roeder says. "It gives a room depth and finish."

Pages 114–115: Sparkling accents, including a diminutive crystal chandelier above this bedroom's vanity and a pair of tall glass table lamps flanking the bed, provide an airy counterpoint to dark-stained furniture and an earthy palette. **Above:** Shimmering silk pillows in colors inspired by the Persian rug lend glamour and shine to this warm, restful room. **Left:** A skirted chair sidling up to the glamorous dressing table introduces feminine charm to this room's rich color palette.

winning
white

White bedrooms get a bad rap, and it's not hard to see why: Many are stark, sterile, and seriously cold. This one defies the stereotype. While it is certainly crisp and clean, it's also warm, inviting, and more than a little quirky. Designers Jim Gauthier and Susan Stacy wanted to keep things light and have some fun. The result is white in a whole new light.

White bedrooms can be dangerous
designwise. "People are rarely comfortable with
an all-white scheme," says interior designer Jim Gauthier.
"White seems too perishable, too easy to get dirty. But in
truth, it's easy to keep fresh and simplifies things. It also
allows furniture shapes to stand out." He, along with Susan
Stacy, proved that point by fashioning this warm, white
bedroom for the Cape Cod Conservatory Showhouse.

The designers chose eclectic furnishings with sensuous
curves and striking lines. Set against white walls, bedding,
and window treatments, the mix shines brightly. The
focal-point bed sets a tone that is both nostalgic and
cutting edge. A driftwood-and-crystal chandelier, a
striped floor, and a sheer and billowy cornice mounted
above the bed lend to the quirky old-new charm, as do

Pages 118–119: White unites disparate furnishings
seamlessly. A ladder-back chair and rustic stool
nestle up to an early-American-style bed and
unmatched contemporary side tables with
unexpected grace. **Opposite:** To make small
bedside windows appear more gracious, Roman
shades hang high and sheers fall to the floor.
Above: A driftwood chandelier, woven sea-grass
bench, and shell studies are reminders of the
room's beachside location.

wall-mounted lamps and quilted slipcovers tied to the
bed's headboard and footboard. "We wanted the room to
feel luxurious and comfortable," Gauthier says. "But we
also wanted it to exude a fun, easygoing vibe in keeping
with the coastal setting and amazing water views."

cool blue getaway

Soothing colors, reflective surfaces, and subtle sheens make this urban loft's master bedroom, which soars high above downtown, feel as though it's adrift in the clouds. Light and airy design touches visually enlarge the small space, capturing the serene spirit of the skies.

The tantalizing blank slate that awaited three designers in the master bedroom of a Little Rock showhouse included a floor-to-ceiling glass wall offering spectacular city views and a black concrete floor that visually grounded the space. "We wanted this space to be tranquil," designer Kevin Walsh says. "And because the room was so small, we knew that meant keeping things very light and very bright."

He and design partners Brett Pitts and Susan Walsh wrapped the room in calming blue. The walls, sheer draperies, and quilted coverlet on the bed are awash in a muted blue; the upholstered headboard and bedskirt are a shade darker. Crisp white linens, white painted bedside tables with mirrored tops, and a striking starburst mirror above the bed create contrast.

The designers' decision to use matching tables and lamps was calculated. "It bolsters the room's sense of order and calm," Kevin Walsh says. The open shelf

Pages 122-123: Sheer draperies that run along a ceiling-mounted track boost the room's quiet luxury. **Opposite:** White accessories, including sculptural coral that appears to float on a Lucite stand, lend a calming influence; touches of black visually ground the setting. **Above left:** The shelving unit functions as a geometric display space; the light wood tone prevents the piece from being obtrusive. **Above:** A sinuous transparent chair helps the small room live larger.

design of the tables, as well as the transparency of the bedside Murano glass lamps, contribute an airy quality in the sun-drenched room.

Even when the sun sets, the room still sparkles. "Showhouse-goers would come in, sigh, and say that they wanted to spend a night here," Susan Walsh says. "And night is the best time of all—the city lights twinkle and the room slips into an even more glamorous mood."

"**Upholstered headboards** are versatile. You can custom-size them to fit your space or add shapes for interest."

—designer KEVIN WALSH

Opposite: Mirrored tabletops and the subtle sheen of the coverlet fabric play an important role in the design. "Their reflectivity adds to the calm, open feel of the space," designer Kevin Walsh says. **This photo:** White tulips echo the room's sculptural accessories in both shape and color.

be my guest

Beautiful guest rooms are acts of kindness. Lovely color, luxurious bedding, good lighting, and accessories that spark the imagination make friends and family feel pampered and comfortable. Guest rooms furnished with a desk, a chair, and a sofa also serve as everyday retreats. You'll feel like a guest in your own home.

graceful restraint

Classic motifs and quiet colors harmonize in this

grandly proportioned bedroom. Wallpaper featuring a timeless damask pattern covers the 10-foot walls to tame the spaciousness and create a welcoming backdrop for fine furnishings with gentle curves and traditional appeal.

Soft shades of green and cream bring
intimacy to this large bedroom. Mirrors and crystal accessories add reflective allure.

Bigger isn't always better, especially when the goal is a bedroom that seemingly wraps its arms around guests. With its 10-foot-tall ceilings and oversize proportions, designers Kevin Walsh, Brett Pitts, and Susan Walsh knew it would take a special effort to rein in the grandness of this guest room in a Little Rock showhouse, and they were up for the challenge.

Using a simple and restrained color palette of soft greens and creams, the design trio ushered the room into a tranquil realm. Walls dressed in English damask wallpaper create intimacy "in a way that paint couldn't," Kevin Walsh says. "And the color is fresh and different."

Rather than filling the large space with an abundance of furnishings and accessories, the designers struck a simplified yet graceful note in the room with just a few perfectly proportioned pieces of furniture. Each well-chosen piece boasts classic good looks and stand-alone appeal. The gently curved upholstered headboard, for example, features deep tufting that lends a cloudlike

Pages 130–131: "Its character gave us direction," designer Kevin Walsh says of the damask-pattern wallpaper. **Above left:** Striped silk cushions add extra comfort and sheen to the bedside chair. **Above right:** Mirrored bedside tables reflect light and bring a glamorous aesthetic to the room. **Opposite:** The chest, which is based on 18th-century commodes, stores clothes, serves as a vanity, and acts as a desk when the writing surface is pulled out. The large-scale Venetian mirror offers the perfect spot for grooming.

softness. The mirrored bedside chests introduce sparkle. "Pulling in a little Hollywood retro glamour added to the elegance of the space," Walsh says.

Other alluring details, including silk-covered buttons on the bedding, striped silk chair cushions, a Venetian mirror, pretty perfume bottles on a silver tray, and crystal lamps, make the room resonate with style without sacrificing restful relaxation.

peaceful privacy

For the ultimate guest getaway, a savvy Florida design couple converted their three-car garage into a stylish guesthouse. A relaxing view of the St. Johns River from the sitting room sets the stage for a serene bedroom featuring vacationlike luxury. Traditional furnishings ground the elegant mood in the past.

Rich fabrics and storied antiques fashion classic comfort in this guest haven.

Pages 134–135: A gilt mirror is simple adornment above the grand carved antique bed. Phoebe Howard dressed the bed in linens and pillows from her retail stores, Mrs. Howard and Max & Co. **Above:** A trunk covered in shells is one of the few items in the quarters reminding guests of their location. A symmetrical arrangement matches artwork for artwork and chair for chair. **Right:** Comfort reigns in the sitting area where an English ottoman with a crewelwork top and a French needlepoint chair contribute pattern and texture.

Helping clients design their guest rooms is part of the job for Jim and Phoebe Howard, an interior designer and decorator, respectively. But the couple's own travels abroad inspired a key element of their Jacksonville, Florida, guesthouse project. "Phoebe and I had gone to France, and one thing we did every night was sit around a fireplace," Jim says. "I wanted the fireplace to be the heart of this space."

With a custom-designed limestone mantel anchoring the cottage's living room, Jim color-washed the walls in shades of terra-cotta, green, and blue. The effect appears as soothing azure, appropriate to the river outside.

For the bedroom proper, the pair created the ultimate sleeping space—untouched by outside light. "Two doors open from the living room, so during the day there is great natural light in the bedroom," Phoebe says. "But at night when you close those doors, it is completely dark in there, which creates a very private and secure feeling."

Furnishings throughout the space mix French and English antiques, mostly in Regency and Empire styles. As expected, such antiques bring stories to share with guests: The pair found the bed in Charleston, South Carolina, and discovered it had originally belonged to John Jacob Astor IV, who died when the Titanic sank.

ageless beauty

Dressed to the nines in luxe linens

and completed with ornate black tole headboards, a pair of twin beds in this guest room makes a stunning statement. The classic furnishings and patterns, which include ticking stripes and florals, ensure that the design stands the test of time.

Ivory walls and fabrics lend
a softer look than true white and
harmonize with the timeworn antiques.

Wanting to create an old-fashioned, collected-over-time look, designer Linda Knight Carr sought inspiration in antiques for this North Carolina guest room. When she discovered a stately antique daybed with matching black tole headboard and footboard, she knew she had found her muse. She split the daybed to create twin beds: The original headboard is on one, and the footboard is reinterpreted as a headboard on the other. The pair shares a single antique nightstand—a smart move where square footage is at a premium.

Carr selected blue-and-cream fabrics in classic motifs to dress the beds, windows, and upholstered furniture. By mixing ticking stripes with three floral patterns, all of which are set against a cream background, Carr kept the look unified and fresh. A few bold splashes of blue from the bedside lamp and the homeowner's collection

Pages 138–139: The pair of tall tole headboards makes a stylish statement in this guest room. The same blue-and-cream toile skirts the beds, dresses the windows, and upholsters the benches at the foot of each bed. **Above:** The distressed finish on the new furniturelike vanity lends an aura of age. **Opposite:** A diminutive antique dresser holds bath linens and guests' clothing. Using just one curtain panel on the corner window keeps the fabric from interfering with the bed.

of Asian pottery keep the otherwise pale color scheme from washing out.

"I wanted to create a bedroom with twin beds elegant enough for a married couple, comfortable enough for children, and stunning enough to be the primary bedroom seen at the top of the staircase," Carr says.

Dainty blue bouquets
repeat throughout the room,
creating a sense of serenity.

This photo: Warm whites mask fingerprints better than true white, making the color palette deceptively practical for visiting grandchildren—especially since nearly all of the fabrics are washable. **Opposite:** A trim settee slips effortlessly into the guest room, thanks to its slim profile and coordinating fabric.

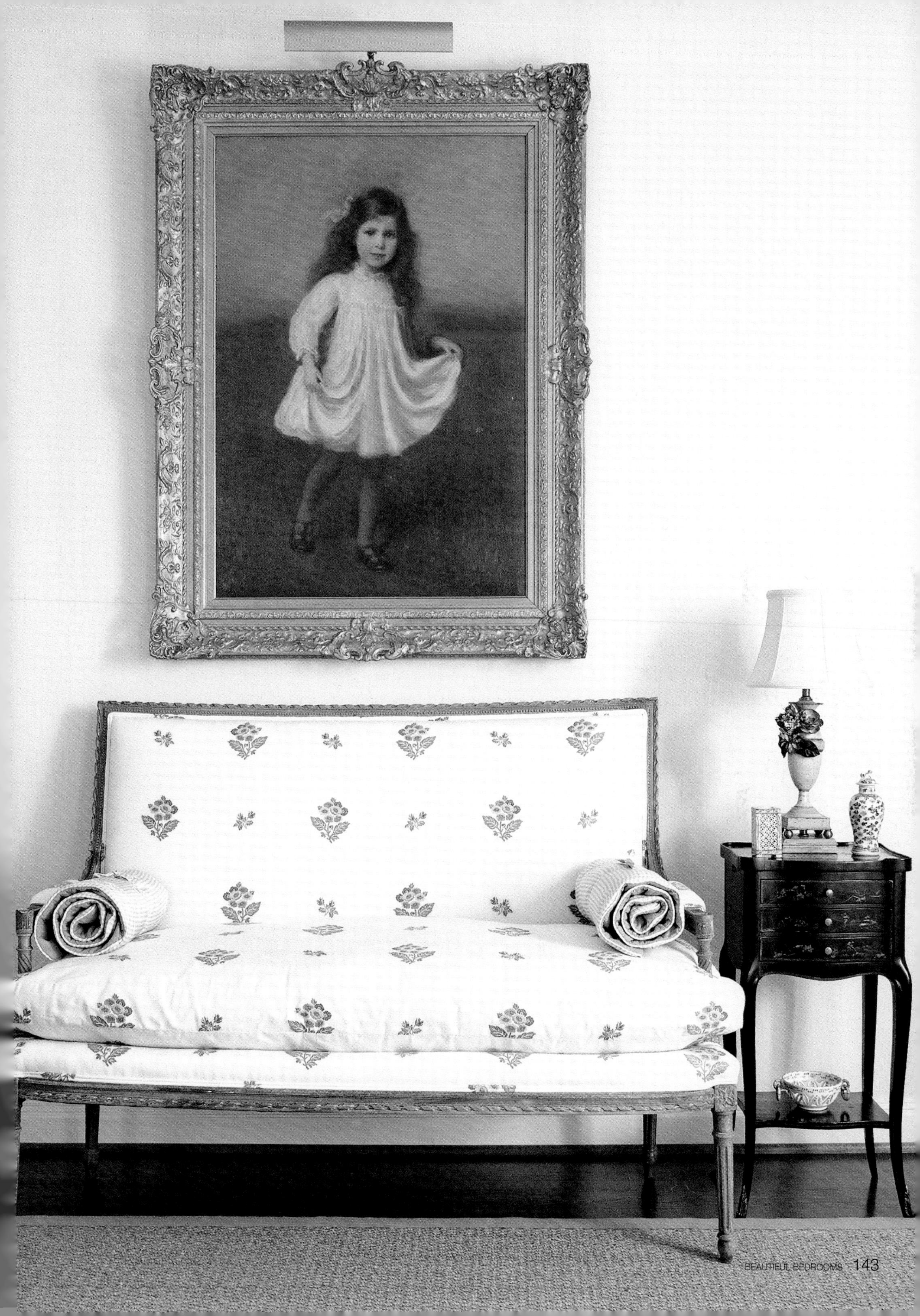

soothing
respite

Serene
relaxation
found in upscale hotels
is re-created in this generously
sized suite. All the elements
are right at hand, from the luxe
headboard upholstered in silk
to the separate sitting space
and elegant bath. Midcentury
bedside tables mingle with
traditional antiques, such as the
grand table at the foot of the bed.

The inviting bed, dressed in shades of cream, champagne, and ivory, sets the color palette.

Pages 144–145: The low headboard of the custom, fully upholstered bed bespeaks the glamorous style associated with high-end hotels. Texture gives the embroidered silk duvet added character in this neutral space. **Above:** The carved French armoire lends the sitting area design gravitas. A pair of upholstered chairs continue the symmetrical balance of the room. **Right:** An elaborate black lacquered Coromandel screen from China has commanding presence set against the room's warm color scheme.

Designed for guests, this luxuriously appointed suite functions as a comfortable home within a home. Charlotte interior designer Teri Thomas made sure of that with the lushly dressed, fully upholstered bed. The inviting rest spot, dressed in shades of cream, champagne, and ivory silk, sets the color palette for the room. In keeping with the serene scheme, Thomas opted to carpet the floor and to dress the window in rolled bamboo blinds and woven drapery panels hung on simple iron rods. She flanked the bed with unexpected contemporary tables that have open shelves for accessories and reading material. Matching lamps create a sense of balance.

The designer worked in plenty of extras, from comfortable seating to unexpected art and accessories. The space boasts its own living area with a writing desk and chair as well as a pair of matching upholstered chairs grouped in front of a carved French armoire. In the bedroom proper, a bench under the Chinese screen and a French-style gilded chair offer stylish extra seating. Also adding to the comfort are a dressing table and the elegant adjoining bath.

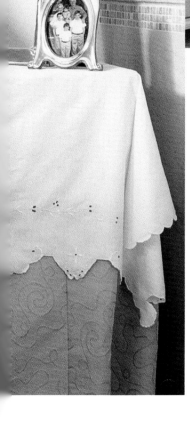

Left: An aged finish enlivens the walls behind the dressing table. The pretty cutwork cloth, small lamps, and framed family photos soften the rustic backdrop. **Above:** The adjacent bath includes a vanity with double sinks, plenty of under-the-counter storage, and a walk-in shower (not shown). **Right:** Garden roses in a silver goblet on the dressing table continue the color scheme.

vintage bright

Keeping both style and scale in mind,

Minneapolis designers Jackie Millea and Jessica Barnd fashion an escape that plays much larger than its Lilliputian dimensions. Period-perfect details combine with lustrous finishes and riotous hues to compose a hospitable haven in tune with the home's early-20th-century architecture.

of vibrant color and sparkling sheen.

Pages 150–151: Cottage-garden harmonies sound a welcoming note in this inviting aerie outfitted with vibrant botanical-motif fabrics and avian-inspired prints. A tone-on-tone wall treatment makes the space seem larger. **Opposite:** A green leather chair, a standing lamp with a turned base, and a leather-top side table—all chosen for their period-apt profiles and compact contours—accommodate a guest's daydreaming and tea-drinking needs. Terra-cotta-color glass knobs carry the main fabric's tawny hues to the built-in cabinetry. **Left:** Crystal accessories echo the wall's pearly luster and the posh sheen of the bed-top textiles—the translucent accents catch the eye without overpowering the diminutive space.

A hand-screened fabric, colored in shades of olive green, terra-cotta, gold, and black, sets an upbeat tempo for this cheerful guest room conversion created by Jackie Millea and Jessica Barnd for the Minneapolis ASID Showcase House. "We wanted the room to be cottage in feeling and work with the 1901 home, but still have a lively energy," Millea says. "The fabric is so fun that we used it to create the room's focal point—the upholstered full-size bed—and repeated it as hourglass window panels that play up the vintage theme."

The walls' alternating matte and pearlescent stripes set off the fabric's lilting hues and supply an architectural counterweight to a wall of built-in cabinets. Making the most of the 13×12-foot room, the designers chose scaled-down reproduction furnishings and sculptural black accents that generate interest without crowding the tiny space. Touchable textiles atop the bed—a silky coverlet, satin sheets, a green chenille blanket, and velvet shams—stage a truly grand and gloriously plush finale.

"Since we couldn't use a lot of patterns in such a small space, we used a variety of textures to boost interest," Millea says. "The luxurious fabrics bring warmth, and their subtle shimmer supports the room's design rhythms. The layers of fabrics make the bed a cushy spot you'll never want to leave!"

unlimited luxury

A guest room offering all the comforts of home may

sound too good to be true. This space, though, embraces its role as a sanctuary for weary travelers. With pampering amenities inspired by European-style boutique hotels, the room is a blissful getaway intended for enjoying peaceful solitude and drifting off to slumber in comfort.

Anyone who has indulged in a stay in a luxury hotel knows how addictive all the amenities are—and how difficult it can be to leave them behind. Los Angeles designer David Dalton wanted houseguests staying in this room to enjoy a similar sense of comfort. He accomplished that, starting with the thing that can make or break a visitor's stay: the bed.

For sink-in comfort, Dalton dressed the bed with a high-quality mattress cover, fluffy featherbed, high-thread-count sheets, soft pillows, and a thick duvet tucked inside a smooth cover. "You can make a bed with such luxury that it's like diving into a cloud—you want to spend all day there," the designer says.

Other thoughtful touches ensure that visitors can complete tasks just as they would in a hotel: without ever leaving their room. The nightstand is actually a desk with enough workspace for a laptop computer. A woven armchair anchors a cozy reading spot. The armoire holds

Pages 154–155: The powder-blue upholstered headboard, aqua walls, and aqua-and-celery striped draperies contribute to the guest room's fresh look. The woven leather bench can hold a breakfast tray or suitcase. **Above left:** The bookcase and other dark-stained pieces anchor the airy setting. Intriguing textures, such as the woven armchair and the split-bamboo armoire, engage the eye. **Above right:** What is a stay in California without sun-worshipping? The balcony beckons with cushioned aluminum chairs featuring a bronze powder-coated finish. **Opposite:** A diminutive upholstered side chair is the perfect height for the writing desk by the bed.

a television and DVD player for watching movies. And the private balcony is replete with cushioned chairs and a chaise longue for basking in the sun. In fact, Dalton created such an inviting space that even the homeowners have been known to check in to their grand guest getaway.

capturing the cape

Inspired by charming seaside cottages, this breezy blue-and-white guest room conjures an atmosphere of pure relaxation. Nostalgic fabrics, natural textures, and well-chosen accessories transport visitors to the seaside. You can almost hear the roar of the surf, smell the saltwater in the air, and feel the warm sand between your toes.

Every day is summer in this sun-kissed guest room inspired by designer Cheryl Stanley's ruminations on classic Cape Cod beach cottages. "I began with the colors of sand, sea, and sky," she says. "They are all soothing and all perfectly suited to any bedroom." Stanley began her work by installing wood-plank walls and painting them soft blue. She then laid a blue-tinged sea-grass rug atop pine floors and paired simple floral drapery panels with textural bamboo shades at the windows. To augment the room's nostalgic beauty, Stanley chose distressed white bedside tables, a vintage floor lamp, and an old-fashioned armoire. Her decision to use sprightly blue-and-white gingham on the bed's simple headboard and matching skirt pours on the charm.

Pages 158–159: Floral panels hang from steel rods mounted high to give the small room a sense of height. A sea-grass rug anchors the bed. **Opposite:** Dark-stained pine floors, bamboo blinds, and wicker picnic baskets provide texture and color contrast in this airy space. **Above:** A bamboo mirror framed by a trio of flea-market platters that echo the drapery and pillow fabrics makes the simple headboard appear grander.

Well-chosen accessories complete this room's beach-house romance. Wicker picnic baskets set beneath the bedside tables, crackled blue-and-white platters framing a bamboo mirror above the headboard, and tall apothecary jars with sand and shells atop the armoire all evoke bygone days, Cape Cod style, and that relaxed feeling of sunshine on your shoulders.

"The light of the sky, the softness of the sand, and the color of the sea all soothe the soul."
—designer CHERYL STANLEY

coastal retreats LINDA LEIGH PAUL   UNIVERSE
THE PACIFIC NORTHWEST AND THE ARCHITECTURE OF ADVENTURE

the perfect wedding DETAILS   McBride-Mellinger   Harper Collins

Opposite: Books and flowers arranged in a bowl echo the simple blue-and-white palette and keep the peace beautifully. A shapely brushed-steel lamp lends a subtle touch of shine. **This photo:** A tall antique-inspired armoire hides the television and opens to drawer storage for clothing.

attic retreat

Recasting a tiny attic as a grand getaway presents challenges and opportunities—most notably in bringing function to what is often an asymmetrical layout. Designer Kimberly Davey's attention to detail and dramatic touches, including a sumptuous canopy that makes good use of a sloped wall, turns what was wasted space into prime real estate.

With the right attitude, anything is possible in decorating. Designer Kimberly Davey wisely looked beyond the gloominess and paltry square footage of an empty attic in a Baltimore showhouse and envisioned the space as an intimate guest bedroom. She imagined the room's dormers, sloped ceilings, and overall angular geometry transformed into cozy, quiet, and functional nooks. "I loved the architectural differences and angles," Davey says.

For the sleeping space, Davey nestled a twin bed in one corner and gave it an illusion of grandeur with a fabric canopy and flowing side panels. Other awkward spaces were transformed with similar aplomb: A boudoir chair and ottoman anchor a steeply sloped corner that serves as a reading nook. A skirted dressing table takes up residence in one dormer; a writing desk, in another. For a bit of stow-everything-in-the-attic whimsy, Davey furnished the space with consignment-shop finds. "Even though the pieces have different finishes, they all flow together," she says.

A harmonious flow is key to the room's enveloping quality. Blue wallpaper covers the walls, and the complementary canopy fabric ensures an uninterrupted visual flow that helps the small space live large.

Pages 164–165: Side panels hung from a rod attached near the ceiling give the bed cozy allure; the fabric behind the bed tacks to the wall. The valance completes the canopylike look. **Above left:** An antique doorknob is cleverly reinterpreted as a holdback for the side panels. **Above right:** An embroidered vanity skirt and a dainty valance made from a tablecloth brighten the blue setting. **Right:** Flirty trims, such as the bullion fringe on the chair and ottoman, give the room its polished style.

rooms to grow

Planned for dreaming and for practicality, children's rooms function best as well-organized spaces that adapt to the rapid changes of early childhood. Airy and bright rooms with simple furnishings translate gracefully as bed and desk replace crib and changing table. Colors and motifs that spark imagination without overwhelming set the happy scene for years to come.

pretty ever after

Luxuriously appointed with upholstered walls, silk draperies, wool carpet, and a chandelier above a round crib that shimmers with sumptuous fabrics, this dreamy pink nursery appears plucked from a fairy tale. Though interior designer Suellen Gregory bestowed this room with happily-ever-after beauty, she also grounded it in practicality. It's a space that will grow up gracefully with the lucky baby who occupies it.

The goal is a space that will grow with the child.

Interior designer Suellen Gregory's client was sure about one thing: She wanted upholstered walls for her daughter's large, high-ceiling nursery. "That decision set the tone for the room," Gregory says. "When you walk in, you feel such warmth and such softness."

Gregory found a beautiful but affordable pink-and-cream floral that complements blue silk window treatments fashioned from voluminous panels left in the house by previous owners. Gently arched silk cornices keep the mood feminine and youthful. "I didn't want the room to feel too grown up," she says.

Gregory did, however, design it with an eye to the future. "The best nurseries grow into the best children's rooms. If you make smart choices, the room will last and last," she says. This room's only ephemeral feature is the luxuriously appointed round crib. An old-fashioned striped silk covers bumpers, and the long skirt is a shimmering pink silk. "Those fabrics were a real splurge," Gregory admits. "But they were definitely worth it."

Pages 170–171: Nostalgic cotton florals upholster padded walls. Because the job required 30-plus yards of fabric, finding a great looking but affordable fabric was key. The armchair is a slipcovered rocker. **Opposite:** Pretty patterned fabric disguises the plumbing; wainscoting marks a transition from white to wallpaper on the walls. **Above left:** An antique engraved vase holds a fresh burst of roses. **Top right:** Striped silk piping and bows adorn the blue silk draperies. **Bottom right:** Baby Chloe's monogram details the fireplace mantel.

global views

Though designed for a young girl, this bedroom's eclectic inspirations crisscross the globe and travel through time. Its exuberant palette of bright coral and even brighter magenta is whimsical, a little wild, and 100 percent smile-inducing.

In planning this joyful girl's bedroom, interior designer Barry Dixon proved one thing outright: Not only do girls want to have fun, sometimes their designers need to cut loose a bit, too. "This room is effusive without being over the top," says Dixon, a Washington, D.C., designer. "Well, maybe it's a little over the top, but it's a girl's room, so it's fine and fabulous."

A saturated coral-and-magenta palette promotes pure bliss that is only slightly sobered by touches of cream and black. The furnishings provide a magic carpet ride to exotic destinations. Fabrics celebrate India with shimmering pattern and embroidery. An upholstered ceiling and walls are swathed in swirling floral vines. What looks like a fluffy dahlia above the tall, slender four-poster is actually an African headdress; a pink pendant recalls the psychedelic '60s, and bombé chests, along with a comfy cut-velvet armchair and a tufted ottoman, are a nod to European tradition. It's a bold and glorious hodgepodge that globe-trots, time-travels, and enchants in original and stylish fashion.

Pages 174–175: Elegant coral sheers romance the bed and soften the windows, where a pair of curvaceous bombé chests provide clothing storage and color relief. **Opposite:** Fashion renderings hang in orderly rows that contrast neatly with the free-form swirl of the upholstered walls and a 1960s-inspired pink pendant. **Above:** Intricate mosaic tiles in the bath conjure exotic Morocco and echo lush colors and shapes from the adjoining girl's bedroom.

cocoon of content

In the microscopic world of insects, there's more going on than meets the eye. The same is true in this bug-theme boy's room, where interior designer Barry Dixon was busy as a bee using earthy colors, natural materials, whimsical furniture, and creative details to create a room that's crawling with fun.

"When I design for kids,
I try to think like a kid. I use more
furniture because they are smaller."

—designer BARRY DIXON

Interior designer Barry Dixon's goal for this insect-theme room was to surround a young boy in contentment. Sandy walls, dark floors overlaid with a soft braided rug, and a cozy built-in bunkbed were just the start.

"When I design for kids, I try to think like a kid," says the Washington, D.C., designer. "I use more furniture because they are smaller. What might feel crowded to adults feels good to children." Using a curved sofa, wicker stools, stackable and easy-to-move chairs, and a six-leg table, Dixon created a gathering spot for homework, games, and puzzles at the center of the bedroom. "Each piece is a little buggy in its lines," he explains.

The windows amplify the room's entomological feel. Khaki linen draperies resembling mosquito net layer over natural woven blinds. That same linen acts as a soft and transparent alternative to a toy-closet door and is used for a panel that draws shut to create semiprivate cubbies of the individual bunks. "Kids love to compartmentalize," Dixon says. "It's the sheet-over-the-dining-room-table thing." Antique science-class posters depicting worms and larvae provide this room's striking finishing touch.

Pages 178–179: Interior designer Barry Dixon chose chairs, a table, and the bamboo bunkbed ladder for their insectlike profiles. Framed beetle prints accessorize the toy-and-television closet. **Opposite:** The adjoining art studio is light and bright with a large armoire for storage. **Above:** The seating area curls up in the room like a caterpillar. Unusual old science-class posters echo the room's earthy palette and insect theme.

circus in town

A charming carnival theme heralds the arrival of a new baby in a welcoming nursery that speaks of fun summer days under the big top. The striped ceiling oversees a detailed room filled with soft colors, a cheerful mix of patterns, and a crib and toy box hand-painted with nostalgic circus scenes.

Pages 182–183: A festive canopy and flying pennant announce the arrival of a new baby. A pretty blend of printed, striped, and checked bedding complements the curved wooden crib. **Opposite:** The designer planned the nursery, with its window seat and child's table and chairs, to be a playroom and gathering spot as well as sleeping space. **Left:** A chandelier with decorative crystals shines under the big-top-painted ceiling. **Below:** A soft gingham fabric translates into cottage-style slipcovers for the armchair and matching ottoman, ideal for curling up at storytime.

This Newport Show House nursery comes complete with one of the most beloved childhood memories—the day the circus came to town. A novelty print fabric with scenes of an old-fashioned country fair set the starting point for designers Roselle McConnell and Ramona Rodger. "Our goal was to create a room that was nostalgic and subtle, yet fun and fresh," McConnell says.

Cream-color wallpaper in stripes and dots contributes an understated backdrop, topped by a ceiling designed to resemble a circus tent. Alternating stripes of rice paper and buttermilk-color paint spread out in rays from a central point above a sparkly chandelier. "Never underestimate the power of the ceiling," McConnell says. The designers repeated the tent motif with a flowing patchwork fabric canopy above the crib. They chose coordinating fabrics in a mélange of checks, stripes, prints, and solids for the many soft goods in the room.

Thoughtful details add interest and finish off the Rhode Island nursery with flair. The crib and toy box sport hand-painted festive fair scenes—children on carousels, whimsical circus animals, and capering clowns. The changing table and pint-size tables and chairs feature floral designs. Above a window seat heaped with pillows, pennants gaily fly over a padded cornice. With interesting details to catch the eye from floor to ceiling, the generous space and quiet palette ensure nursery fun for both baby and parents for now and through childhood.

prep cool

Inspired by classic preppy style of the 1940s, interior designer Kelley Proxmire gave an undistinguished girl's room a retro-chic makeover where damask looks dynamite, checks are chic, and grandmother's frumpy draperies assume a new cool. Unexpected gold and acrylic accents make the room shine.

Some things old, some things new, and plenty of fresh blue add up to a room that's a joy to be in and built to last.

Pages 186–187: An antique clock, vanity mirror, and headboards echo the damask wallpaper's curvaceous shapes. The small-check duvets on the beds play cheerfully to the larger check on the vanity table skirt. **Opposite:** The vanity table's sparkling lamps, mirrored tabletop, and haute couture acrylic chair give this fresh-scrubbed room a touch of glamour. **Left and below:** Vintage dark wood furniture, including a small table between the beds and a chest of drawers, took on a Scandinavian accent when designer Kelley Proxmire painted them cool gray.

A wave of sentimentality washed over interior designer Kelley Proxmire when she discovered the bold-scale blue-and-white damask paper that covers the walls of this charming girl's room. "It reminded me of 1940s wallpaper in my aunt and uncle's Maryland country house," Proxmire says. "On one hand, it was wonderfully nostalgic, but on the other, it had major impact."

Proxmire used that wallpaper to give a plain room fanciful new personality and a sense of architecture, which she built upon with shapely matelassé-upholstered headboards. She then dressed the windows with old-fashioned white silk draperies and valances combined with unexpected white woven blinds. The unusual pairing warms the room and breathes in freshness, but serves another purpose as well: It hides unattractive metal window frames. A gray wash used to refinish a chest of drawers, nightstand, and chandelier provides muted contrast to bold blue walls. "I didn't want white or wood," Proxmire says. "This finish was cool and vaguely Scandinavian." While silver accents would have worked beautifully here, Proxmire opted for bright gold instead. "Not only was it less expected, it was warmer and gave the room drama," she says.

resources

The Suite Life

Fresh Tradition

finishing touch

Sweet slumber beckons under the cocooning comfort of a canopy. Let a romantic crown be a dramatic final statement.